CHURCH
ON
TRIAL

STUDY GUIDE

STUDY GUIDE

CHURCH
ON
TRIAL

How to **protect** your congregation,
mission, and reputation **during a crisis**

PHIL COOKE

AVAIL

CONTENTS

PART 1

CREATING A POSITIVE CULTURE AS A DEFENSE AGAINST A CRISIS

1

WHAT DO PEOPLE THINK OF WHEN THEY THINK OF YOU?

Managing perceptions isn't about ego or manipulation; it's about creating an environment where you and your organization are appreciated, not just tolerated.

As you read
Chapter 1:
"What Do
People Think
of When
They Think
of You?" in
Church on Trial,
review, reflect
on, and respond
to the text by
answering
the following
questions.

REFLECT AND TAKE ACTION:

How can you effectively manage the perception of your church in the community, ensuring that the positive aspects of your mission are accurately conveyed?

_____

_____

_____

_____

_____

What steps can you take to address and rectify negative perceptions or rumors about your church or its members?

_____

_____

_____

_____

_____

How can you balance the need for authenticity with the necessity of managing public perception, avoiding the pitfalls of seeming manipulative or insincere?

_____

_____

_____

_____

_____

_____

> *Now when they saw the boldness of Peter and John, and perceived that they were uneducated, common men, they were astonished. And they recognized that they had been with Jesus.*
>
> **—Acts 4:13 (ESV)**

Consider the scripture above and answer the following questions:

What does this scripture reveal to you about perception?

_____

_____

_____

_____

_____

_____

_____

_____

What can you learn from Jesus's approach to managing public perception, and how can these principles be applied to your modern church leadership?

_____

_____

_____

_____

_____

_____

_____

_____

In what ways can you use modern media and emotional storytelling to enhance your church's message and connect with a broader audience?

_____

_____

_____

_____

_____

_____

_____

_____

_____

_____

How can you ensure that your church's perceived image aligns with its core values and mission, and what checks can be implemented to monitor this alignment continuously?

_____

_____

_____

_____

_____

_____

_____

_____

_____

_____

2

YOUR CHURCH OR MINISTRY CULTURE MATTERS

Whether you lead a church, ministry, or nonprofit, the best possible way to avoid a crisis is by building a healthy culture.

As you read
Chapter 2:
"Your Church
or Ministry
Culture
Matters" in
Church on Trial,
reflect on,
and respond
to the text by
answering
the following
questions.

REFLECT AND TAKE ACTION:

How can you proactively create a healthy
and biblical culture within your church or
ministry to prevent potential crises?

_____

_____

_____

_____

_____

_____

_____

_____

What steps can you take to ensure that issues
or unusual behaviors within your church
or ministry are appropriately reported and
addressed before they escalate into larger
problems?

_____

_____

_____

_____

_____

_____

_____

_____

_____

_____

How can you balance being supportive and understanding of staff members with the need to address potential red flags that may indicate underlying problems?

_____

_____

_____

_____

_____

_____

_____

_____

_____

_____

What measures can you implement to educate your staff and congregation about the dangers of technology and pornography, and how can you monitor and safeguard your church's digital environment?

_____

_____

_____

_____

_____

_____

_____

_____

_____

How can you develop a culture of trust, transparency, and mutual accountability among your church or ministry team members?

_____

_____

_____

_____

_____

_____

_____

_____

_____

_____

What strategies can you employ to cultivate leadership development, ensuring that potential leaders within your church or ministry are identified, equipped, and deployed effectively?

_____

_____

_____

_____

_____

_____

_____

_____

_____

_____

3

IT CAN HAPPEN TO ANYONE, ANYTIME

Disaster can happen. Actually, you should plan that a disaster will happen.

READING TIME

As you read
Chapter 3:
"It Can Happen
to Anyone,
Anytime" in
Church on Trial,
reflect on,
and respond
to the text by
answering
the following
questions.

REFLECT AND TAKE ACTION:

Do you have a comprehensive crisis management plan in place? If so, when was the last time it was reviewed and updated to address new potential threats, such as cyber fraud and online misconduct?

_____

_____

_____

_____

_____

_____

_____

_____

What systems of accountability do you have for monitoring staff behavior and financial transactions? Are these systems sufficient to detect and prevent issues like embezzlement, fraud, or inappropriate relationships?

_____

_____

_____

_____

_____

_____

_____

_____

_____

How well-prepared is your church for potential legal challenges? Have you consulted legal experts to ensure your policies and practices comply with current laws and regulations, particularly regarding issues like property disputes, personal injuries, and zoning?

_____

_____

_____

_____

_____

_____

_____

_____

With the rise of digital surveillance and data breaches, what steps are you taking to protect the privacy and integrity of your staff and congregants? Are you aware of the potential risks associated with personal devices and social media usage by staff members?

_____

_____

_____

_____

_____

_____

_____

_____

_____

What ongoing training do you provide to your staff and volunteers to recognize and respond to signs of misconduct or crisis situations? How do you ensure that everyone understands the importance of reporting unusual or suspicious behavior immediately and appropriately?

_____

_____

_____

_____

_____

_____

_____

_____

_____

_____

FOR LEADERS, ACCOUNTABILITY STARTS ON DAY ONE

Take responsibility whether you're responsible for it or not . . . If you can't handle it, then you need to look for another job.

READING TIME

As you read
Chapter 4:
"For Leaders,
Accountability
Starts on
Day One" in
Church on Trial,
reflect on,
and respond
to the text by
answering
the following
questions.

REFLECT AND TAKE ACTION:

When you step into a new leadership role, how do you ensure you fully assume responsibility and accountability from day one? What immediate actions do you take to address and communicate your commitment to solving existing organizational problems?

_____

_____

_____

_____

_____

_____

_____

What strategies have you implemented to shift your organization's culture that may have been problematic under previous leadership? How do you measure progress and ensure that these strategies are effectively driving change?

_____

_____

_____

_____

_____

_____

_____

_____

What personal accountability measures have you put into place to safeguard against potentially risky behaviors? Do you have a trusted mentor, peer, or accountability partner who provides oversight and honest feedback on your actions?

_____

_____

_____

_____

_____

_____

_____

_____

_____

How do you respond to crises, both big and small, within your organization? What steps do you take to publicly address significant issues, and how do you ensure that your response builds trust and demonstrates leadership?

_____

_____

_____

_____

_____

_____

_____

_____

_____

What proactive steps can you take to manage and mitigate risky behaviors, such as inappropriate internet use, alcohol consumption, or financial mismanagement?

_____

_____

_____

_____

_____

_____

_____

_____

_____

_____

In today's connected, social media-driven world, how do you maintain transparency and honesty in your leadership? What measures do you take to ensure that your actions, both private and public, uphold the integrity and trust expected from a church leader?

_____

_____

_____

_____

_____

_____

_____

_____

_____

_____

5

A ONE-TIME CRISIS VERSUS A CULTURE OF ABUSE

In abusive cultures, there are problems underneath the surface just waiting to bubble up.

READING TIME

As you read
Chapter 5:
"A One-Time
Crisis Versus
a Culture of
Abuse" in
Church on Trial,
reflect on,
and respond
to the text by
answering
the following
questions.

REFLECT AND TAKE ACTION:

How do you differentiate between a one-time crisis and signs of a deeper, ongoing culture of abuse within your church? What specific behaviors or patterns do you look for in leaders and staff that may indicate a toxic environment?

_____

_____

_____

_____

_____

_____

_____

_____

_____

How do you ensure that all staff members feel safe to voice their concerns and know they will be heard and addressed?

_____

_____

_____

_____

_____

_____

_____

_____

How do you hold leaders, including yourself, accountable for their behavior and interactions with staff and congregation members? What mechanisms are in place to address and rectify instances of abuse or misconduct swiftly and effectively?

_____

_____

_____

_____

_____

_____

_____

_____

_____

How accessible are you and your leadership team to the congregation? What practices do you follow to ensure that leaders remain connected and responsive to the needs and concerns of church members?

_____

_____

_____

_____

_____

_____

_____

_____

_____

In what ways do you balance the influence of charismatic leaders to prevent them from overstepping boundaries or creating a personality-driven culture? How do you ensure that the church's mission and values remain central rather than being overshadowed by individual leaders?

_____

_____

_____

_____

_____

_____

_____

_____

_____

How do you teach and model a biblical understanding of honor and authority within your church? What safeguards are in place to prevent the misuse of these concepts to justify abusive behavior or create a hierarchical, fear-based culture?

_____

_____

_____

_____

_____

_____

_____

_____

_____

WHEN *HONOR* GOES TOO FAR

"Honor" does not mean looking the other way and allowing a leader complete freedom. Sometimes, it means respectful disagreement.

As you read
Chapter 6:
"When *Honor*
Goes Too
Far" in
Church on Trial,
reflect on,
and respond
to the text by
answering
the following
questions.

REFLECT AND TAKE ACTION:

How do you define "honor" within your church? What guidelines or principles do you have in place to ensure that honor toward leaders does not become excessive or lead to a culture of forced loyalty?

_____

_____

_____

_____

_____

_____

_____

_____

How do you create an environment where respectful disagreement is encouraged and valued? What processes are in place to ensure that team members feel safe to voice their concerns or disagreements without fear of retribution?

_____

_____

_____

_____

_____

_____

_____

_____

How do you balance showing respect to pastoral authority with maintaining accountability?

_____

_____

_____

_____

_____

_____

_____

_____

_____

_____

What steps do you take to prevent the development of a leader-centered culture where the focus revolves too much around a single person? How do you promote a culture that emphasizes the collective mission and vision of the church rather than individual personalities?

_____

_____

_____

_____

_____

_____

_____

_____

_____

_____

How do you handle pastor appreciation and gifts from the congregation? What criteria do you use to determine what is appropriate, and how do you ensure that gifts do not signal or lead to undue influence or favoritism?

_____

_____

_____

_____

_____

_____

_____

_____

_____

_____

What signs or behaviors do you consider as red flags indicating that honor may be going too far? How can you address these issues promptly and effectively to prevent a culture of unhealthy or excessive honor from taking root in your church?

_____

_____

_____

_____

_____

_____

_____

_____

_____

_____

WELCOME TO THE CHRISTIAN ATTACK CULTURE

The choice is ours. We can use the internet to build up or use it to tear down.

READING TIME

As you read
Chapter 7:
"Welcome to the
Christian Attack
Culture" in
Church on Trial,
reflect on,
and respond
to the text by
answering
the following
questions.

REFLECT AND TAKE ACTION:

How does your church currently handle criticism on social media and other online platforms? Do you have a protocol for determining when to respond and when to let criticism go unanswered? (If not, we'll cover this in Chapter 26.)

_____

_____

_____

_____

_____

_____

_____

_____

What strategies do you employ to encourage constructive and respectful dialogue within your church community, both online and offline? How do you model this behavior as a leader?

_____

_____

_____

_____

_____

_____

_____

_____

_____

Do you offer training or resources to your congregation on how to engage online in a Christ-like manner? How do you educate your members about the potential impact of their online interactions?

_____

_____

_____

_____

_____

_____

_____

_____

_____

How do you balance the need for transparency and addressing public concerns with the importance of private, personal reconciliation and correction? What steps do you take to ensure issues are handled appropriately before they escalate?

_____

_____

_____

_____

_____

_____

_____

_____

_____

How do you monitor and address potential red flags on social media that might indicate deeper issues within your church community, such as patterns of negativity or the emergence of serious accusations?

_____

_____

_____

_____

_____

_____

_____

_____

_____

_____

What initiatives do you have in place to create a positive and uplifting online presence for your church?

_____

_____

_____

_____

_____

_____

_____

_____

_____

_____

8

THE ELEPHANT IN THE ROOM

When it comes to the workplace, there are plenty of elephants in plenty of rooms, and few people seem to have the courage to point them out.

READING TIME

As you read
Chapter 8:
"The Elephant
in the Room" in
Church on Trial,
reflect on,
and respond
to the text by
answering
the following
questions.

REFLECT AND TAKE ACTION:

Are there any persistent issues or behaviors within your church or ministry that staff members are aware of but hesitant to discuss openly? What are some steps you can take to encourage open dialogue about these issues?

_____

_____

_____

_____

_____

_____

_____

_____

_____

How do you create a safe and trusting environment where staff members feel comfortable bringing up difficult or sensitive topics? What measures can you implement to ensure confidentiality and protection for those who speak up?

_____

_____

_____

_____

_____

_____

_____

_____

_____

Have you assessed whether any of your leadership practices might inadvertently contribute to a culture of silence or fear? How can you modify these practices to promote transparency and accountability?

_____

_____

_____

_____

_____

_____

_____

Are there historical issues or "elephants" that have been around for a long time and continue to affect your church's culture and operations? How can you start addressing these issues constructively and inclusively?

_____

_____

_____

_____

_____

_____

_____

Do you clearly communicate the negative impact of ignoring the above "elephants," such as loss of trust, decreased morale, or financial losses? How can you quantify and present these consequences to highlight the importance of addressing the issues?

_____

_____

_____

_____

_____

_____

_____

_____

_____

Do you cast vision for the positive result of removing the elephant? How can you clearly share the benefits of addressing the problem?

_____

_____

_____

_____

_____

_____

_____

Once an "elephant" is successfully addressed, how do you recognize and celebrate the efforts of the team involved? How can you ensure that credit is shared and that the process encourages future openness and problem-solving?

_____

_____

_____

_____

_____

_____

_____

9

IMMORALITY AND THE POWER OF A GLASS DOOR

If you're a leader, the cost of switching your office doors isn't nearly as expensive as the cost of making the mistake of a lifetime.

READING TIME

As you read
Chapter 9:
"Immorality
and the Power
of a Glass
Door" in
Church on Trial,
reflect on,
and respond
to the text by
answering
the following
questions.

REFLECT AND TAKE ACTION:

Do your office spaces currently promote transparency and accountability? What steps can you take to install glass doors or windows in your offices to ensure visibility and prevent inappropriate behavior?

_____

_____

_____

_____

_____

_____

_____

_____

How do you currently monitor the interactions between staff members, particularly those of the opposite sex? Are there clear guidelines and boundaries in place to prevent the development of inappropriate relationships?

_____

_____

_____

_____

_____

_____

_____

_____

_____

> *The eyes of the LORD are in every place,*
> *keeping watch on the evil and the good.*
>
> **—Proverbs 15:3 (ESV)**

Consider the scripture above and answer the following questions:

What is the meaning of this verse, and how can you apply it to how you lead?

_____

_____

_____

_____

_____

_____

_____

_____

Beyond physical changes to the office environment, what additional preventative measures can you implement to address the risk of moral failings among your staff? This could include regular training on professional boundaries and ethical behavior.

_____

_____

_____

_____

_____

_____

_____

_____

As a leader, how do you model moral integrity and transparency in your daily interactions? What practices can you adopt to set a positive example for your team in maintaining professional boundaries?

_____

_____

_____

_____

_____

_____

_____

_____

_____

_____

10

THE TOP SIX HABITS OF PASTORS IN TROUBLE

These risky behaviors can sometimes go on for years, but I've noticed that at least one of them is almost always in play at the time of a pastor's downfall.

READING TIME

As you read
Chapter 10:
"The Top
Six Habits
of Pastors in
Trouble" in
Church on Trial,
reflect on,
and respond
to the text by
answering
the following
questions.

REFLECT AND TAKE ACTION:

How do you monitor and address alcohol
or substance use among your pastoral
staff? Are there clear guidelines in place to
promote responsible behavior, especially
when attending conferences or events?

_____

_____

_____

_____

_____

_____

_____

_____

What measures are in place to ensure
that interactions and humor among
staff members remain professional and
respectful? How do you address instances of
inappropriate behavior or jokes within the
workplace?

_____

_____

_____

_____

_____

_____

_____

_____

How do you promote healthy work-life balance among pastoral staff, particularly concerning time spent away from spouses or family members? Are there policies in place to prevent excessive time apart and potential risks to marital relationships?

_____

_____

_____

_____

_____

_____

_____

_____

_____

What steps are taken to address issues of pornography or inappropriate online behavior among leaders? Are there support systems or accountability measures in place to assist those struggling with addiction to digital content?

_____

_____

_____

_____

_____

_____

_____

_____

_____

How do you cultivate a culture of accountability where leaders feel comfortable questioning decisions or behaviors that may be concerning? What mechanisms are in place to ensure that concerns are addressed promptly and effectively?

_____

_____

_____

_____

_____

_____

_____

_____

_____

_____

PART 2

PART 2

HOW TO RESPOND
TO A CRISIS

BUILD A CRISIS COMMUNICATION TEAM AND PLAN

Long before a crisis happens, I recommend selecting your crisis communication team.

As you read
Chapter 11
"Build a Crisis
Communi-
cation Team
and Plan" in
Church on Trial,
reflect on,
and respond
to the text by
answering
the following
questions.

REFLECT AND TAKE ACTION:

How will you select members for your crisis communication team, considering factors such as expertise, experience, and availability? What criteria will you use to ensure the team is well-rounded and effective?

_____

_____

_____

_____

_____

_____

_____

_____

Who will serve as the primary spokesperson for your organization during a crisis? What qualities and qualifications are essential for an effective spokesperson, and how will you prepare them for this role?

_____

_____

_____

_____

_____

_____

_____

_____

_____

Have you considered providing media training for potential spokespersons within your organization? How will you ensure they are equipped to handle media interviews and press conferences with confidence and professionalism?

_____

_____

_____

_____

_____

_____

_____

_____

_____

Do you have a designated command center or crisis management room prepared for use during emergencies? What facilities and resources will be essential for effective crisis coordination, communication, and decision-making?

_____

_____

_____

_____

_____

_____

_____

_____

_____

How will you ensure the privacy and security of sensitive information and discussions within your command center? What measures will be put in place to restrict access and maintain confidentiality during crisis response efforts?

_____

_____

_____

_____

_____

_____

_____

_____

How will you balance the demands of crisis response with the need to maintain regular operations within your church or ministry? What strategies will you implement to ensure continuity of essential services and activities during times of crisis?

_____

_____

_____

_____

_____

_____

_____

_____

_____

CREATING A CRISIS COMMUNICATIONS PLAN

The heart of your crisis response is your church or ministry communication director.

READING TIME

As you read
Chapter 12:
"Creating a
Crisis Com-
munications
Plan" in
Church on Trial,
reflect on,
and respond
to the text by
answering
the following
questions.

REFLECT AND TAKE ACTION:

What specific vulnerabilities does your church or ministry face, and how can you anticipate potential crises in these areas?

_____

_____

_____

_____

_____

_____

_____

_____

How does your current budget impact your ability to respond to a crisis effectively? What steps can you take now to improve your financial preparedness and ensure adequate resources are available to manage potential crises in the future?

_____

_____

_____

_____

_____

_____

_____

_____

_____

What security measures do you currently have in place to protect your staff, congregation, and facilities? How can you enhance your security protocols, including the installation of fencing, security cameras, and exterior lighting, to mitigate potential risks?

_____

_____

_____

_____

_____

_____

_____

Does your staff have adequate training in crisis communication? How can you provide communication training or access to communication consultants to ensure your team is prepared to communicate effectively during a crisis?

_____

_____

_____

_____

_____

_____

_____

Do you have a comprehensive social media strategy in place to communicate with your congregation and the public during a crisis? Elaborate on your strategy.

_____

_____

_____

_____

_____

_____

_____

_____

What can you do to cultivate positive relationships with the media to ensure accurate reporting and effective communication during a crisis?

_____

_____

_____

_____

_____

_____

_____

What next steps do you need to take to create a simple and easy to activate crisis communication plan in the event of a crisis?

_____

_____

_____

_____

_____

_____

_____

13

WHEN A CRISIS HAPPENS, DON'T WAIT TO ACT

It's been said that good generals plan for battle, but great generals plan for the unexpected.

REFLECT AND TAKE ACTION:

READING TIME

As you read
Chapter 13:
"When a Crisis
Happens, Don't
Wait to Act" in
Church on Trial,
reflect on,
and respond
to the text by
answering
the following
questions.

How can you shift your mindset from reacting to crises as they occur to proactively preparing for potential crises before they happen? What steps can you take now to ensure readiness and resilience in the face of unexpected challenges?

_____

_____

_____

_____

_____

_____

_____

What lessons can you glean from the experiences shared in this chapter, such as the tragic outcome of the Donner Party, to inform your approach to crisis management? How can you avoid repeating the mistakes of those who failed to act swiftly in the face of impending crises?

_____

_____

_____

_____

_____

_____

_____

What are the potential consequences of waiting too long to intervene in a crisis situation? How can you overcome the tendency to delay action due to concerns about reputation, congregational attitude, or fear of making mistakes?

_____

_____

_____

_____

_____

_____

_____

_____

_____

How can you cultivate a culture of attentiveness to red flags that may indicate the early stages of a crisis? What processes can you implement to encourage staff and leaders to report concerns promptly, allowing for timely intervention and resolution?

_____

_____

_____

_____

_____

_____

_____

_____

_____

What strategies can you employ to balance the need for timely intervention with the importance of gathering sufficient information before taking action? How can you ensure that your responses are well-informed and measured, even in the midst of urgency?

_____

_____

_____

_____

_____

_____

_____

_____

_____

_____

How can you empower church leaders and staff at all levels to take swift and decisive action when confronted with a potential crisis? What training, resources, and support systems can you put in place to equip individuals to respond effectively in high-pressure situations?

_____

_____

_____

_____

_____

_____

_____

_____

_____

14

THE BIG PICTURE OF DEALING WITH A CRISIS

During a crisis, leaders don't have to be perfect and don't have to know everything, but they need to inspire confidence.

As you read
Chapter 14:
"The Big Picture
of Dealing with
a Crisis" in
Church on Trial,
reflect on,
and respond
to the text by
answering
the following
questions.

REFLECT AND TAKE ACTION:

How can you instill in your leadership team the understanding that it's not a matter of if a crisis will occur, but when it will happen, and how can you ensure they are adequately prepared for such eventualities?

_____

_____

_____

_____

_____

_____

_____

_____

What steps can you take to educate your staff and leaders about the potential impact of their social media presence on the church's reputation, and how can you mitigate the risks of inappropriate behavior or comments online?

_____

_____

_____

_____

_____

_____

_____

_____

_____

How do you plan to integrate the advice of legal counsel and communication professionals into your crisis response strategy, and what criteria will you use to identify qualified professionals in these areas to support your church or ministry?

_____

_____

_____

_____

_____

_____

_____

_____

_____

In light of the ever-evolving news cycle and social media landscape, how will you determine the optimal timing for responding to crises, especially considering the potential consequences of premature or delayed reactions?

_____

_____

_____

_____

_____

_____

_____

_____

_____

What strategies will you employ to discern between legitimate criticism that warrants a response and online attacks or "trolling" that may be best ignored or addressed offline? How can you maintain perspective and focus on long-term goals amidst the noise of social media backlash?

_____

_____

_____

_____

_____

_____

_____

_____

_____

How can you draw insights from case studies like Jack Graham's handling of a crisis to inspire confidence in your leadership team and cultivate a culture of trust and resilience within your church or ministry? What lessons can you apply from these examples to enhance your crisis management approach?

_____

_____

_____

_____

_____

_____

_____

_____

_____

15

DISASTERS RARELY HAPPEN BECAUSE OF ONE MISTAKE

If we only look for the big mistakes,
we may never find the answers.

READING TIME

As you read Chapter 15: "Disasters Rarely Happen Because of One Mistake" in *Church on Trial,* reflect on, and respond to the text by answering the following questions.

REFLECT AND TAKE ACTION:

How can you encourage your leadership team to adopt a mindset of anticipating potential crises by recognizing the cumulative impact of small mistakes, and what strategies can you implement to proactively address these issues before they escalate?

_____

_____

_____

_____

_____

_____

_____

_____

What steps will you take to cultivate and maintain a strong reputation for your church or ministry, understanding that a positive reputation serves as a crucial asset during times of crisis?

_____

_____

_____

_____

_____

_____

_____

How do you plan to effectively communicate the positive impact of your church's outreach programs, charitable initiatives, and community engagement efforts to both your congregation and the broader public? What platforms and channels will you utilize to share these stories authentically and effectively?

_____

_____

_____

_____

_____

_____

_____

_____

_____

How can you shift the perception of marketing within your church community from mere self-promotion to a strategic approach aimed at expanding the reach and impact of your ministry's mission? What biblical principles can guide your efforts to share your good works with humility and authenticity?

_____

_____

_____

_____

_____

_____

_____

_____

_____

How can you maintain transparency and openness to build trust with both supporters and critics alike?

_____

_____

_____

_____

_____

_____

_____

_____

_____

_____

How will you ensure that your reputation-building efforts align with your values and mission, serving as a foundation for crisis response and recovery?

_____

_____

_____

_____

_____

_____

_____

_____

_____

_____

16

WHAT *NOT* TO DO IN A CRISIS

At the start of a crisis, know there will be plenty of time later to examine what went wrong or assign blame.

READING TIME

As you read
Chapter 16:
"What *Not*
to Do in a
Crisis" in
Church on Trial,
reflect on,
and respond
to the text by
answering
the following
questions.

REFLECT AND TAKE ACTION:

How will you ensure that your leadership
team remains focused on addressing the
immediate concerns of a crisis without
becoming sidetracked by speculation
or blame during the initial phase of the
response?

_____

_____

_____

_____

_____

_____

_____

How do you plan to accurately identify
and understand the specific needs and
expectations of your audience—whether
it's your congregation, supporters, donors,
or the general public—when crafting crisis
communications? What strategies will you
employ to tailor your messages accordingly?

_____

_____

_____

_____

_____

_____

_____

In the event of a crisis, how will you strike a balance between providing spiritual guidance and offering practical assurances to address the concerns and inquiries of your congregation, partners, supporters, and the broader community? How can you ensure that both aspects are addressed effectively?

_____

_____

_____

_____

_____

_____

_____

_____

_____

What measures will you implement to prevent inappropriate or tone-deaf responses to crises, such as offering solely spiritual reassurances in situations requiring practical assurances or vice versa? How will you ensure that your responses resonate with the specific context and nature of the crisis?

_____

_____

_____

_____

_____

_____

_____

_____

_____

How will you equip your leadership team to respond to crises with a professional and strategic approach, considering the importance of addressing the core issues at hand while maintaining transparency, credibility, and trust with your various stakeholders?

_____

_____

_____

_____

_____

_____

_____

_____

_____

In the event of a crisis involving a senior pastor or key spiritual leader, how will you ensure continuity of spiritual leadership and pastoral care for your congregation during the transition period? What steps will you take to provide immediate support and guidance to those affected by the crisis?

_____

_____

_____

_____

_____

_____

_____

_____

_____

_____

17

HOW TO STOP UNWANTED SPECULATION AND RUMOR

When leaders and their organizations are transparent, there's little place left for rumor.

READING TIME

As you read Chapter 17: "How to Stop Unwanted Speculation and Rumor" in Church on Trial, reflect on, and respond to the text by answering the following questions.

REFLECT AND TAKE ACTION:

How can you foster a culture of transparency within your church leadership, particularly in times of crisis, to effectively address speculation and rumor with honesty and integrity?

_____

_____

_____

_____

_____

_____

_____

_____

What strategies can you employ to balance the imperative of telling the truth during a crisis with the need to be sensitive to potentially damaging or unproven information that could harm reputations?

_____

_____

_____

_____

_____

_____

_____

_____

How can you draw inspiration from biblical examples, such as Peter's handling of Judas's betrayal, to guide your approach to crisis communication, emphasizing truthfulness while avoiding unnecessary sensationalism or graphic details?

_____

_____

_____

_____

_____

_____

_____

_____

_____

How can you ensure that the language used in your crisis responses or statements is clear, honest, and accurately reflects the situation, avoiding the pitfalls of euphemisms or misleading terminology that can exacerbate misunderstandings or fuel speculation?

_____

_____

_____

_____

_____

_____

_____

_____

_____

In what ways can you leverage the expertise of professional communicators or public relations specialists to enhance your church's crisis communication strategy, particularly in crafting messages that effectively address speculation and rumor with transparency and authenticity?

_____

_____

_____

_____

_____

_____

_____

_____

How can you demonstrate to your congregation and community that your commitment to truthfulness and transparency during a crisis is not only a reflection of your integrity but also serves to instill confidence in your leadership and the stability of your church's response to challenging situations?

_____

_____

_____

_____

_____

_____

_____

_____

18

WHEN A SENIOR PASTOR OR MINISTRY LEADER EXPERIENCES A MORAL FAILURE

Seeking God is essential in a crisis, but along with that process, there are some immediate practical choices that have to be made.

REFLECT AND TAKE ACTION:

READING TIME

As you read Chapter 18: "When a Senior Pastor or Ministry Leader Experiences a Moral Failure" in *Church on Trial*, reflect on, and respond to the text by answering the following questions.

How have you ensured that your church or ministry is prepared with a crisis management plan to effectively respond to situations such as moral failures among senior pastors or ministry leaders?

_____

_____

_____

_____

_____

_____

_____

_____

What immediate steps will you take to engage legal counsel upon discovering a moral failure involving a senior pastor or ministry leader, particularly concerning legal obligations such as reporting to authorities, especially in cases involving minors?

_____

_____

_____

_____

_____

_____

_____

_____

How will you approach the delicate balance between promptly informing both the authorities and the congregation about a moral failure, considering the potential impact on trust and the need for transparency within the church community?

_____

_____

_____

_____

_____

_____

_____

_____

_____

What strategies will you employ to uphold principles of transparency and honesty in communicating with the congregation about a moral failure while also ensuring that sensitive details are handled with care to avoid unnecessary harm?

_____

_____

_____

_____

_____

_____

_____

_____

_____

How will you leverage the expertise of crisis communication professionals to guide your church's response to a moral failure, particularly in crafting official statements, managing media inquiries, and navigating the complexities of public perception and reputation management?

_____

_____

_____

_____

_____

_____

_____

_____

_____

_____

19

THE FIRST FORTY-EIGHT HOURS AFTER A LEADER'S MORAL FAILURE

Making the wrong decisions during that initial time frame can be very difficult to fix down the road.

READING TIME

As you read
Chapter 19:
"The First
Forty-Eight
Hours After a
Leader's Moral
Failure" in
Church on Trial,
reflect on,
and respond
to the text by
answering
the following
questions.

REFLECT AND TAKE ACTION:

What specific actions do you plan to take within the first forty-eight hours after discovering a leader's moral failure, considering the urgency and potential impact on your organization's reputation and trust?

_____

_____

_____

_____

_____

_____

_____

_____

_____

How do you intend to involve legal counsel promptly to navigate the legal implications and obligations associated with the leader's misconduct, especially concerning issues like mandatory reporting and potential criminal liabilities?

_____

_____

_____

_____

_____

_____

_____

Can you outline your strategy for activating and coordinating a crisis response team to handle the situation effectively, ensuring that key stakeholders are informed and prepared to address evolving developments?

_____

_____

_____

_____

_____

_____

_____

_____

_____

How will you mitigate the risk of engaging in speculation or premature judgment regarding the cause of the leader's moral failure during the critical initial phase, focusing instead on immediate response and damage control?

_____

_____

_____

_____

_____

_____

_____

_____

_____

What measures will you implement to offer support, counseling, and assistance to individuals who come forward as accusers or victims in cases of leader misconduct, recognizing the potential power dynamics and emotional impact involved?

_____

_____

_____

_____

_____

_____

_____

_____

_____

Given the situation, how do you plan to address the presence of the leader's content, such as books, sermons, and videos, within the organization, considering the potential implications for the organization's reputation and credibility?

_____

_____

_____

_____

_____

_____

_____

_____

_____

_____

2 0

WHAT ABOUT THE BOOKS AND TEACHING RESOURCES OF FALLEN PASTORS AND LEADERS?

*No matter how much effort it takes,
focus on the future, not the past.*

REFLECT AND TAKE ACTION:

As you read
Chapter 20:
"What About
the Books
and Teaching
Resources
of Fallen
Pastors and
Leaders?" in
Church on Trial,
reflect on,
and respond
to the text by
answering
the following
questions.

What steps will you take to ensure the swift removal of all materials associated with the fallen leader from your organization's bookstore, online platforms, and social media channels to prevent any negative associations or criticisms?

_____

_____

_____

_____

_____

_____

_____

_____

_____

_____

_____

_____

_____

_____

_____

_____

_____

_____

_____

_____

How will you communicate the importance of focusing on the organization's future rather than dwelling on the past, especially regarding decisions related to the removal of resources associated with the fallen leader?

_____

_____

_____

_____

_____

_____

_____

_____

_____

How do you advise individual believers and followers of the fallen leader to peruse their personal libraries and resources, considering factors such as the severity of the leader's moral failure and the value of the content created before the fall?

_____

_____

_____

_____

_____

_____

_____

_____

_____

In cases where the fallen leader's teachings were considered insightful and valuable before their moral failure, how will you guide individuals in discerning whether to retain or discard such content for personal use and study?

_____

_____

_____

_____

_____

_____

_____

_____

_____

_____

_____

21

WHEN SEX OFFENDERS COME TO CHURCH

It's a new world out there.
Proceed with caution.

As you read
Chapter 21:
"When Sex
Offenders Come
to Church" in
Church on Trial,
reflect on,
and respond
to the text by
answering
the following
questions.

REFLECT AND TAKE ACTION:

How do you plan to educate your pastoral team and other leaders about the nuances and complexities involved in dealing with registered sex offenders attending church services?

_____

_____

_____

_____

_____

_____

_____

_____

What guidelines will you establish for disclosing information about sex offenders to relevant church leaders while ensuring confidentiality and minimizing the risk of legal repercussions?

_____

_____

_____

_____

_____

_____

_____

_____

How will you collaborate with local law enforcement and probation officers to ensure that sex offenders attending your church are compliant with legal requirements and are actively participating in rehabilitation efforts?

_____

_____

_____

_____

_____

_____

_____

_____

How do you intend to tailor your approach to integrating sex offenders into church life based on the specific circumstances and severity of each individual's offense?

_____

_____

_____

_____

_____

_____

_____

_____

_____

What measures will you implement to provide accountability and supervision for sex offenders participating in church activities, particularly those involving interactions with children and vulnerable individuals?

_____

_____

_____

_____

_____

_____

_____

_____

_____

In what ways will you ensure that your church's crisis response team is equipped and ready to act swiftly in the event of any allegations or incidents involving sex offenders violating established principles or committing new offenses?

_____

_____

_____

_____

_____

_____

_____

_____

_____

_____

PUBLIC STATEMENTS AND PRESS RELEASES

For many communication professionals, public statements, crisis statements, and press releases are almost interchangeable, but on closer inspection, they serve distinct purposes.

READING TIME

As you read
Chapter 22:
"Public
Statements
and Press
Releases" in
Church on Trial,
reflect on,
and respond
to the text by
answering
the following
questions.

REFLECT AND TAKE ACTION:

How will you distinguish between
press releases and public statements
in your church's communication
strategy, particularly regarding positive
announcements versus responses to crises?

_____

_____

_____

_____

_____

_____

_____

_____

What initiatives or events within your
church would benefit from press releases as
a means of sharing positive news and stories
with the wider community, and how do you
plan to ensure their effective distribution?

_____

_____

_____

_____

_____

_____

_____

_____

In what circumstances do you anticipate needing to issue public statements, especially in response to crises or sensitive issues, and how will you ensure that these statements effectively address the situation at hand?

_____

_____

_____

_____

_____

_____

_____

_____

_____

_____

How do you intend to leverage social media platforms alongside press releases and public statements to maximize the reach and impact of your church's communication efforts, particularly on today's digital landscape?

_____

_____

_____

_____

_____

_____

_____

_____

_____

_____

Besides issuing press releases, what complementary strategies and tactics will you employ to ensure that your church's key messages and announcements receive adequate media attention and engagement?

_____

_____

_____

_____

_____

_____

_____

_____

_____

Who within your church leadership team will be responsible for consulting communication professionals and accessing online resources to ensure that press releases and public statements are effectively crafted and distributed when needed?

_____

_____

_____

_____

_____

_____

_____

_____

_____

PART 3

WHEN THINGS GET DIFFICULT

23

THE POWER OF ADMITTING YOUR MISTAKES

At the appropriate time, getting the right story out there is absolutely crucial.

As you read
Chapter 23:
"The Power of
Admitting Your
Mistakes" in
Church on Trial,
reflect on,
and respond
to the text by
answering
the following
questions.

REFLECT AND TAKE ACTION:

How can church leaders cultivate a culture of honesty and transparency within their ministry, drawing from examples like Patrick Doyle's admission of mistakes at Domino's Pizza to build trust and credibility?

_____

_____

_____

_____

_____

_____

_____

In cases where church leaders face unwarranted criticism or public scrutiny, what steps should be taken to ensure that the true narrative is communicated effectively, and how can leaders navigate the balance between defending their reputation and demonstrating humility?

_____

_____

_____

_____

_____

_____

_____

_____

When confronted with challenges or failures within the ministry, how can leadership resist the temptation to shift blame onto others and instead take ownership of the situation, acknowledging their role as leaders and the accountability that comes with it?

_____

_____

_____

_____

_____

_____

_____

_____

_____

_____

What strategies can you and your team employ to prevent the accumulation of resentment among your congregation or team members, particularly when mistakes are made, and how can leaders foster an environment where accountability is embraced rather than feared?

_____

_____

_____

_____

_____

_____

_____

_____

_____

_____

How should church leaders navigate situations where personal struggles or family issues intersect with their leadership role? What principles should guide their response to ensure integrity and trustworthiness are maintained?

_____

_____

_____

_____

_____

_____

_____

_____

_____

In what ways can you leverage moments of adversity or failure as opportunities for personal and organizational growth, and how can you encourage a culture where mistakes are seen as learning opportunities rather than causes for shame or blame?

_____

_____

_____

_____

_____

_____

_____

_____

_____

WHEN YOU RECEIVE UNWANTED MESSAGES FROM AN "ADMIRER"

The bottom line is that today, what you consider friendship and what someone else considers friendship may be completely different things.

READING TIME

As you read
Chapter 24:
"When You
Receive
Unwanted
Messages from
an 'Admirer'" in
Church on Trial,
reflect on,
and respond
to the text by
answering
the following
questions.

REFLECT AND TAKE ACTION:

What practical steps can you take to set clear boundaries for your own and your team's digital communication to mitigate the risk of receiving unwanted messages or attention from admirers?

_____

_____

_____

_____

_____

_____

_____

_____

How should you navigate the delicate balance between addressing unwanted messages from admirers and avoiding inadvertently encouraging further communication, especially when the sender is a member of the congregation or someone known to your team?

_____

_____

_____

_____

_____

_____

_____

In light of the potential risks associated with receiving unwanted attention, what accountability measures should you implement within your ministry team to ensure that such incidents are handled appropriately and transparently?

_____

_____

_____

_____

_____

_____

_____

_____

When faced with persistent or serious unwanted messages, what steps should you take to seek legal advice and guidance from media professionals to protect both your personal integrity and the reputation of your ministry?

_____

_____

_____

_____

_____

_____

_____

_____

_____

How can you and your team navigate the blurred boundaries between social media friendships and personal relationships, particularly when faced with requests from individuals you have not met in person or whose intentions may not be clear?

_____

_____

_____

_____

_____

_____

_____

_____

_____

What role can you and your team play in educating your congregation about appropriate digital communication etiquette, particularly emphasizing the importance of respecting personal boundaries and avoiding behavior that could be perceived as harassment or intrusion?

_____

_____

_____

_____

_____

_____

_____

_____

2 5

HOW TO HANDLE INTERVIEWS WITH SECULAR REPORTERS

*If the reporter stops asking questions,
then you stop answering.*

As you read
Chapter 25:
"How to Handle
Interviews
with Secular
Reporters" in
Church on Trial,
reflect on,
and respond
to the text by
answering
the following
questions.

REFLECT AND TAKE ACTION:

How do you discern whether responding to a media request is necessary for your situation?

_____

_____

_____

_____

_____

_____

_____

_____

_____

_____

What criteria should you consider when deciding whether to accept or decline a media interview?

_____

_____

_____

_____

_____

_____

_____

_____

_____

_____

How can you effectively balance the potential benefits and risks of engaging with secular reporters?

_____

_____

_____

_____

_____

_____

_____

_____

_____

Are there specific circumstances in which you feel obligated to respond to media requests, regardless of personal preference?

_____

_____

_____

_____

_____

_____

_____

_____

_____

_____

_____

What strategies can you employ to ensure that your decision regarding media interviews aligns with your organizational values and goals?

_____

_____

_____

_____

_____

_____

_____

_____

_____

_____

How do you determine the level of preparation needed before participating in a media interview to ensure a successful outcome?

_____

_____

_____

_____

_____

_____

_____

_____

_____

_____

2 6

SHOULD YOU RESPOND TO SOCIAL MEDIA CRITICS?

Remember, you don't have to respond.

READING TIME

As you read
Chapter 26:
"Should You
Respond to
Social Media
Critics?" in
Church on Trial,
reflect on,
and respond
to the text by
answering
the following
questions.

REFLECT AND TAKE ACTION:

How do you determine the legitimacy of
criticism received on social media platforms,
especially when considering a response?

_____

_____

_____

_____

_____

_____

_____

_____

_____

_____

What strategies can you employ to manage
your emotional response when faced with
criticism on social media?

_____

_____

_____

_____

_____

_____

_____

_____

_____

When faced with criticism, what factors should you consider before deciding whether or not to respond publicly?

_____

_____

_____

_____

_____

_____

_____

_____

_____

_____

In what instances is it appropriate to engage with social media critics directly, and how can you ensure constructive dialogue?

_____

_____

_____

_____

_____

_____

_____

_____

_____

_____

_____

How can you differentiate between valid criticism that warrants reflection and action and baseless criticism that can be disregarded?

_____

_____

_____

_____

_____

_____

_____

_____

_____

_____

What steps can you take to minimize the potential negative impact of social media criticism on your reputation and organization while still upholding transparency and accountability?

_____

_____

_____

_____

_____

_____

_____

_____

_____

_____

_____

WHEN *CANCEL CULTURE* COMES TO YOUR CHURCH

*Leaders who have the courage to stand
by their convictions and express those
convictions in a compelling way, with grace,
will be the ones much more likely to survive.*

As you read
Chapter 27:
"When *Cancel
Culture*
Comes to Your
Church" in
Church on Trial,
reflect on,
and respond
to the text by
answering
the following
questions.

REFLECT AND TAKE ACTION:

How do you define cancel culture, and what are some of the key characteristics of this phenomenon?

_____

_____

_____

_____

_____

_____

_____

_____

_____

_____

What are some examples of situations where cancel culture has impacted churches or Christian ministries?

_____

_____

_____

_____

_____

_____

_____

_____

_____

In what ways has cancel culture affected the broader cultural landscape, and what are the implications for churches and Christian leaders?

_____

_____

_____

_____

_____

_____

_____

_____

_____

_____

How do you distinguish between legitimate criticism and instances of cancel culture?

_____

_____

_____

_____

_____

_____

_____

_____

_____

_____

_____

What biblical principles can guide church leaders in responding to cancel culture while remaining faithful to their convictions?

_____

_____

_____

_____

_____

_____

_____

_____

_____

_____

How can churches and Christian ministries prepare themselves to navigate potential encounters with cancel culture, both proactively and reactively?

_____

_____

_____

_____

_____

_____

_____

_____

_____

_____

_____

2 8

THE DOMINO EFFECT: THE PTL NETWORK AND HILLSONG CHURCH

The domino effect happens when a single event exposes what can often be a long list of hidden problems that, when revealed, can be devastating.

As you read
Chapter 28:
"The Domino
Effect: The
PTL Network
and Hillsong
Church" in
Church on Trial,
reflect on,
and respond
to the text by
answering
the following
questions.

REFLECT AND TAKE ACTION:

What are some key similarities between the crises faced by PTL Network and Hillsong Church, and what lessons can you learn from these situations?

_____

_____

_____

_____

_____

_____

_____

_____

In what ways do financial mismanagement, leadership issues, and personal scandals contribute to the domino effect observed in both of the above cases?

_____

_____

_____

_____

_____

_____

_____

_____

_____

How can churches ensure they have sufficient safeguards in place to prevent similar crises from occurring within their own organizations?

_____

_____

_____

_____

_____

_____

_____

_____

_____

What role does character assessment play in selecting and vetting church leaders, especially considering the potential impact of personal integrity on organizational stability?

_____

_____

_____

_____

_____

_____

_____

_____

_____

When facing a crisis, what steps can you and your team take to maintain transparency, address concerns, and rebuild trust within your congregation and community?

_____

_____

_____

_____

_____

_____

_____

_____

_____

_____

Considering the potential impact of negative publicity on a church's reputation, what factors should leaders consider when deciding whether to rebrand or rename their organization?

_____

_____

_____

_____

_____

_____

_____

_____

_____

_____

2 9

BEFORE YOU CIRCLE
THE WAGONS

*Before spiritual leaders fall, why doesn't
their inner circle hold them accountable?*

REFLECT AND TAKE ACTION:

READING TIME

As you read
Chapter 29:
"Before You
Circle the
Wagons" in
Church on Trial,
reflect on,
and respond
to the text by
answering
the following
questions.

How does the dynamic between spiritual leaders and their inner circle differ from that of secular leaders? How might this influence accountability within the church?

_____

_____

_____

_____

_____

_____

_____

_____

_____

What are the potential risks of loyalty to a spiritual leader overshadowing the responsibility to hold them accountable for inappropriate behavior or ethical lapses?

_____

_____

_____

_____

_____

_____

_____

_____

In what ways can church leaders create a culture of accountability within their inner circles while still honoring the positive impact spiritual leaders may have had on individuals' lives?

_____

_____

_____

_____

_____

_____

_____

_____

_____

Considering the potential loss of influence or reputation that may result from holding a spiritual leader accountable, what steps can individuals within the inner circle take to prioritize integrity over personal gain?

_____

_____

_____

_____

_____

_____

_____

_____

_____

_____

_____

Reflecting on the warning signs discussed in this chapter, what practical measures can church leaders implement to cultivate an environment where accountability is valued and maintained within the organization?

_____

_____

_____

_____

_____

_____

_____

_____

_____

_____

PART 4

HOW TO POSITION YOUR CHURCH, MINISTRY, OR NONPROFIT FOR THE FUTURE

3 0

TODAY, EVERYONE IS A PR PERSON

Today, because of the power of social media, everyone is a PR person.

As you read
Chapter 30:
"Today,
Everyone Is a
PR Person" in
Church on Trial,
reflect on,
and respond
to the text by
answering
the following
questions.

REFLECT AND TAKE ACTION:

How can you develop an effective strategy for utilizing social media to communicate messages and engage with your audience?

_____

_____

_____

_____

_____

_____

_____

_____

In what ways can you educate your leadership team and influencers about the importance of their social media presence and the potential impact of their posts on the church or ministry's reputation?

_____

_____

_____

_____

_____

_____

_____

_____

_____

What steps can you take to align your vision for social media with the overall goals and mission of your organization?

_____

_____

_____

_____

_____

_____

_____

_____

_____

_____

Considering the accessibility of social media platforms to individuals at all levels of your organization, how can you ensure that everyone understands their role as a "PR person" and the responsibility that comes with it?

_____

_____

_____

_____

_____

_____

_____

_____

_____

_____

How can you identify and leverage the influence of individuals within your team who may not hold traditional leadership roles but have significant reach on social media?

_____

_____

_____

_____

_____

_____

_____

_____

_____

_____

What are some practical ways you can empower your team members to use social media effectively as a tool for sharing important messages and engaging with the community?

_____

_____

_____

_____

_____

_____

_____

_____

_____

_____

3 1

DOES KEEPING QUIET HELP?

Organizations that ignore problems and don't speak up don't last long in a crisis.

As you read
Chapter 31:
"Does Keeping
Quiet Help?" in
Church on Trial,
reflect on,
and respond
to the text by
answering
the following
questions.

REFLECT AND TAKE ACTION:

How do you strike a balance between staying quiet initially and eventually addressing a crisis in a timely manner?

_____

_____

_____

_____

_____

_____

_____

_____

What strategies can you use to effectively utilize social media during a crisis to communicate with the public and share your plan for resolution?

_____

_____

_____

_____

_____

_____

_____

_____

_____

_____

How do you address accusations of hiding the truth or covering up information during a crisis?

_____

_____

_____

_____

_____

_____

_____

_____

_____

What steps can you take to ensure transparency while protecting the privacy of victims and sensitive information?

_____

_____

_____

_____

_____

_____

_____

_____

_____

_____

After a crisis, what strategies can you implement to manage online search results and minimize the visibility of negative content?

_____

_____

_____

_____

_____

_____

_____

_____

_____

_____

How can you leverage positive stories and content to counteract negative information and maintain a positive online presence?

_____

_____

_____

_____

_____

_____

_____

_____

_____

_____

_____

3 2

BE MORE CAREFUL SENDING EMAILS!

*Start by burning this into your memory:
never say anything in an email you would
not want to be shouted from the housetops.*

READING TIME

As you read
Chapter 32:
"Be More
Careful Sending
Emails!" in
Church on Trial,
reflect on,
and respond
to the text by
answering
the following
questions.

REFLECT AND TAKE ACTION:

How can you raise your team's awareness
of the potential risks associated with email
communication, especially regarding privacy
and confidentiality?

_____

_____

_____

_____

_____

_____

_____

_____

_____

What steps can you take to ensure that
everyone on your team understands the
importance of exercising caution when
sending emails?

_____

_____

_____

_____

_____

_____

_____

_____

_____

In what ways can you implement policies or guidelines to mitigate the risk of inappropriate or damaging content being shared via email?

_____

_____

_____

_____

_____

_____

_____

_____

_____

_____

How can you encourage a culture of accountability and responsibility among team members regarding their email communication?

_____

_____

_____

_____

_____

_____

_____

_____

_____

_____

What training programs or resources can you provide to equip your team with the knowledge and skills necessary to use email effectively and responsibly?

_____

_____

_____

_____

_____

_____

_____

_____

_____

_____

How can you emphasize the importance of face-to-face communication for sensitive or critical matters rather than relying solely on email?

_____

_____

_____

_____

_____

_____

_____

_____

_____

_____

3 3

JACK HAYFORD AND THE POWER OF LOCAL MEDIA

*Couldn't the Church use a little positive
coverage in the media for a change?*

As you read
Chapter 33:
"Jack Hayford
and the Power
of Local
Media" in
Church on Trial,
reflect on,
and respond
to the text by
answering
the following
questions.

REFLECT AND TAKE ACTION:

How can you proactively engage with local media outlets to build positive relationships and amplify your church's message?

_____

_____

_____

_____

_____

_____

_____

_____

_____

What steps can you take to reach out to reporters covering religious events in your community while offering assistance and insight into Christian topics?

_____

_____

_____

_____

_____

_____

_____

_____

_____

_____

What lessons can you learn from Jack Hayford's approach to engaging with the media, and how can you apply them to enhance your church's influence in your local area?

_____

_____

_____

_____

_____

_____

_____

_____

_____

How do you prioritize building relationships with local journalists as part of your church's outreach strategy?

_____

_____

_____

_____

_____

_____

_____

_____

_____

_____

In what ways can you change the narrative surrounding Christianity in the media by fostering constructive dialogue and offering valuable insights to reporters?

_____

_____

_____

_____

_____

_____

_____

_____

_____

_____

How might positive coverage of your church in local media outlets contribute to a more favorable perception of Christianity in your community?

_____

_____

_____

_____

_____

_____

_____

_____

_____

_____

34

PAST SIN DOES NOT MAKE YOU A BETTER SPIRITUAL LEADER

Never fall for the deception that your past sin makes you more effective as a Christian leader.

READING TIME

As you read
Chapter 34:
"Past Sin Does
Not Make You a
Better Spiritual
Leader" in
Church on Trial,
reflect on,
and respond
to the text by
answering
the following
questions.

REFLECT AND TAKE ACTION:

How do you prevent the misconception
that past sins automatically enhance your
effectiveness as a spiritual leader?

_____

_____

_____

_____

_____

_____

_____

_____

What steps can you take to ensure continual
personal growth and improvement as a
leader, irrespective of past experiences?

_____

_____

_____

_____

_____

_____

_____

_____

_____

How do you balance acknowledging past mistakes while understanding that they do not define your present or future leadership capabilities?

_____

_____

_____

_____

_____

_____

_____

_____

In what ways can you actively engage in the restoration and accountability process rather than seeking shortcuts or bypassing essential steps?

_____

_____

_____

_____

_____

_____

_____

What measures can you implement to uphold integrity and authenticity in your leadership role, regardless of past failings or shortcomings?

_____

_____

_____

_____

_____

_____

_____

_____

_____

Who are the trusted individuals or mentors in your life who can provide accountability and guidance as you navigate the complexities of leadership and personal growth?

_____

_____

_____

_____

_____

_____

_____

_____

How can you ensure receptivity to constructive feedback and support, particularly during times of vulnerability or temptation?

_____

_____

_____

_____

_____

_____

_____

3 5

TOWARD THE FUTURE: WORKING WITH A PUBLICIST

Whether you've been through a crisis or want to get more positive stories about your church, ministry, or specific project out there in the media, you may want to consider an ongoing relationship with a public relations firm or a publicist.

As you read
Chapter 35:
"Toward
the Future:
Working with
a Publicist" in
Church on Trial,
reflect on,
and respond
to the text by
answering
the following
questions.

REFLECT AND TAKE ACTION:

How can you establish a collaborative partnership with a publicist or PR firm to effectively convey your message to the public?

_____

_____

_____

_____

_____

_____

_____

_____

_____

What strategies can you and your team employ to create engaging content in collaboration with the publicist, aligning with your mission and target audience?

_____

_____

_____

_____

_____

_____

_____

_____

_____

How can you and your team leverage existing church platforms, such as social media and radio programs, to complement the efforts of the publicist and maximize outreach opportunities?

_____

_____

_____

_____

_____

_____

_____

_____

_____

_____

What is a realistic timeline for seeing tangible results from the publicity campaign, and how can you maintain perseverance in the face of setbacks or rejections?

_____

_____

_____

_____

_____

_____

_____

_____

_____

_____

How can you and your team avoid taking rejection or criticism from media outlets personally, focusing instead on constructive feedback and opportunities for improvement?

_____

_____

_____

_____

_____

_____

_____

_____

_____

_____

In what ways can you and your team remain open to diverse interview opportunities and unconventional media platforms, recognizing their potential for broader impact and unexpected connections?

_____

_____

_____

_____

_____

_____

_____

_____

_____

_____

3 6

IT'S TIME TO RAISE THE BAR ON MARRIAGE

If the Christian community worked harder to make our marriages and families succeed, it would have an enormous impact nationwide.

As you read
Chapter 36:
"It's Time to
Raise the Bar
on Marriage" in
Church on Trial,
reflect on,
and respond
to the text by
answering
the following
questions.

REFLECT AND TAKE ACTION:

How can you prioritize biblical teaching on marriage within your church or ministry, considering its significant impact on individuals and families?

_____

_____

_____

_____

_____

_____

_____

_____

In what ways can your team integrate spouses into the ministry work, echoing the example set by organizations like the Salvation Army, and fostering a culture that values marital partnership?

_____

_____

_____

_____

_____

_____

_____

_____

_____

What steps can you and your team take to ensure that spouses of ministry leaders are included in work-related travel opportunities, promoting unity and shared experiences within marriages?

_____

_____

_____

_____

_____

_____

_____

_____

_____

How can your church actively cultivate a reputation as a marriage-friendly church or ministry, ensuring that both single and married individuals feel valued and supported in their spiritual journey?

_____

_____

_____

_____

_____

_____

_____

_____

_____

_____

As leaders, how can you and your team set a strong example of marital commitment and family unity, recognizing the profound impact it can have on your witness in today's culture?

_____

_____

_____

_____

_____

_____

_____

_____

_____

Considering the importance of marriage counseling and support groups within the church, what initiatives can you undertake to strengthen marriages and families within your congregation and beyond?

_____

_____

_____

_____

_____

_____

_____

_____

_____

37

CAN YOU AVOID A FULL-BLOWN CRISIS?

Ultimately, it's an individual question, and each of us has to answer it for ourselves.

READING TIME

As you read
Chapter 37:
"Can You Avoid
a Full-Blown
Crisis?" in
Church on Trial,
reflect on,
and respond
to the text by
answering
the following
questions.

REFLECT AND TAKE ACTION:

How can you integrate transparency into
your organization's culture, particularly
regarding office design and accessibility?

_____

_____

_____

_____

_____

_____

_____

_____

_____

What strategies can you and your team
implement to avoid situations that may
compromise integrity, such as traveling
with individuals of the opposite sex without
additional employees present?

_____

_____

_____

_____

_____

_____

_____

_____

_____

How can you establish multiple filters for handling finances within your organization to mitigate the risk of financial misconduct?

_____

_____

_____

_____

_____

_____

_____

_____

_____

What steps can you take to ensure that private communication channels, such as email, are used responsibly and in alignment with organizational values?

_____

_____

_____

_____

_____

_____

_____

_____

_____

How can you and your team implement web filtering software to address the risks associated with pornography in the workplace?

_____

_____

_____

_____

_____

_____

_____

_____

_____

_____

How might you adapt the principles of Billy Graham's Modesto Manifesto, particularly regarding interactions with members of the opposite sex, to align with the needs and context of your organization while maintaining integrity?

_____

_____

_____

_____

_____

_____

_____

_____

_____

_____

SUMMARY: WHEN A CRISIS HAPPENS

When a crisis does happen, panic often ensues, and that's the moment a true leader can make a positive impact.

READING TIME

As you read
"Summary:
When a Crisis
Happens" in
Church on Trial,
reflect on,
and respond
to the text by
answering
the following
questions.

REFLECT AND TAKE ACTION:

How can you ensure that your crisis communication plan is up-to-date and readily accessible in times of need?

_____

_____

_____

_____

_____

_____

_____

_____

What steps can you take to establish an effective command center for managing crises and ensuring privacy and security?

_____

_____

_____

_____

_____

_____

_____

_____

_____

How can you balance the need to act quickly with the imperative of transparency during a crisis?

_____

_____

_____

_____

_____

_____

What strategies can you implement to prioritize empathy and compassion towards those affected by the crisis?

_____

_____

_____

_____

_____

_____

What measures can you take to monitor media coverage of the crisis and respond promptly to any inaccuracies or misrepresentations?

_____

_____

_____

_____

_____

_____